THE RENAISSANCE

THE LIVING PAST

Between 1300 and 1600 life in Europe went through
enormous changes. It was a new age of thinking and
learning and it is called the Renaissance. It was
a time of astonishing inventions in the world of
science; printing was developed; discoveries in
astronomy were made; daring men set out to explore
uncharted seas and there were exciting advances in
painting, sculpture, architecture, and literature.
But it was also an age of violence, poverty,
squalor and disease. This beautifully illustrated
book gives a fascinating account of the
events, the places and the lives of the people
of the Renaissance age.

ARCO PUBLISHING, INC.
New York

Published by Arco Publishing, Inc.
219 Park Avenue South, New York, N.Y. 10003

© Marshall Cavendish Limited 1979 — 1984

Printed and bound in Hong Kong by
Dai Nippon Printing Company

This volume is not to be sold in Australia or
New Zealand

Library of Congress Cataloging in Publication Data

Goodenough, Simon.
    The Renaissance.

    (The Living past)
    Bibliography: p.
    Includes index.
    SUMMARY: Presents an account of life during
the Renaissance, a period which profoundly influenced
the development of European civilization.
    1.   Renaissance—Juvenile literature.
(1.   Renaissance) I. Title.
CB361.G66   1979   909'.4   79–10210
ISBN 0-668-04787-9

Acknowledgements

Author:
Simon Goodenough
Adviser:
Margaret Walker Hannan
Editor:
Jane Sheard
Art Editor:
John Curnoe
Designer:
Jacky Paynter
Picture Researchers:
Linda Proud
Julia Calloway

Illustrations

Vivienne Brown 26-27, 34-35; Pat Casey 20-21; Peter Glazier 22-23, 24-25; John Green/John Martin and Artists Ltd. 14-15; Richard Hook 17; John Hunt/John Martin and Artists Ltd. Front cover, 31; Gary Rees/Linda Rogers Associates 32-33, 40-41; Juan Wijngaard 8-9, 18-19.

Pictures

Ashmolean Museum 12-13, 18-19; Bodleian Library 6(L); Reproduced by permission of the British Library 18, 33; Cooper-Bridgeman Library 43(B), 44(R); Reproduced by Gracious Permission of Her Majesty Queen Elizabeth II 6 (R), 36 (B); Giraudon 26, 27 (TR), 41 (L), 45 (T), 53 (BR); Herzog August Bibliothek 30 (B); By courtesy of the Italian State Tourist Office (E.N.I.T.) 51; Mansell Collection 31, 52 (L & TR), 53 (L), 55 (TC), 57 (B);

The Metropolitan Museum of Art, Rogers Fund, 1919, The Harvesters by Pieter Breughel the Elder 22-23; Courtesy of the Trustees of the National Gallery 12, 44(L), 45(B); National Gallery of Art, Washington, 13 (Widener Collection, Francesco Sforza by Francesco Bonsignori), 14 (Samuel H. Kress Collection, Lorenzo de Medici by Andrea del Verrochio), 15(C) (Samuel H. Kress Collection, Lorenzo and Giuliano de Medici, Obv. bust of Lorenzo by Bertoldi di Giovanni), 15(B) (Samuel H. Kress Collection, Lorenzo and Giuliano de Medici, rev. bust of Lorenzo); Radio Times Hulton Picture Library 27(L & BR), 52(BR); Ann Ronan Picture Library 36(T), 37; Scala 2, 4, 7, 8, 9, 10-11, 15(T), 16, 20, 21, 24, 25, 28, 29, 20(T), 34, 35, 38, 39, 41(R), 42, 43(T), 46, 47, 49, 49, 50, 52(C), 53(TR), 54, 55(L, BC & R), 56, 57(T), endpapers.

Contents

The Great Revival

The word *renaissance* means rebirth, and the years between the 14th and 16th centuries are known as the Renaissance because the scholars and artists of the time were trying to revive the glories of Greek and Roman civilization.

After the collapse of the great Roman Empire there had been a long period of warring throughout Europe. Education and learning had been forgotten in the struggle to survive. People accepted their fate, obeyed the Church and their masters without question and had no curiosity about the world around them. The men of the Renaissance called this period the Dark Ages.

But in the 14th century, Europe was politically more stable. Governments gradually became secure. People could begin to build up trade and accumulate wealth. In a more settled society, some people began to compare their way of thinking with the beliefs of classical writers. It was particularly exciting for the Italians because their country had once been the heart of the world's greatest empire. It was almost like discovering their family history. They were very much aware that they lived in a special and exciting age.

The scholars who studied the classical works wanted people to be aware of the beauty in themselves and in nature so that they would worship God more fully.

Wealthy people encouraged sculptors and painters to put these ideas into art. For the first time in centuries artists began to portray people and other living things in a lifelike way.

But the Renaissance was also a time of contrast. Society as a whole changed very slowly. Outside the densely packed towns and cities there were vast areas of scarcely populated countryside. The peasants on the land lived a harsh life, far from the feasts and tournaments of the rich and the merchants' moneybags.

Even such great events as the discovery of America or the realization that the Earth was not the centre of the universe were hardly heard of, let alone understood, by most people.

But the spirit of confidence and enquiry that characterized the Renaissance started to affect ordinary people too. Peasants rebelled against lords and kings; humble priests spoke out against the wealth and power of the Pope in Rome. People became more aware of themselves as individuals and of their right to have, and speak, their opinions.

Below left: A plant study painted before the Renaissance: the berries are not very realistic.

Below right: Wild flowers painted by Leonardo have been studied very carefully.

Right: A poet is crowned with laurels in the splendour of a Renaissance palace.

Town and Country

Most of the excitement and activity during the Renaissance was in the cities and towns. The countryside was used only by princes for hunting, by the peasants for farming and by soldiers for a battlefield. It was in the towns that princes had their palaces, the merchants had their banks and that trade was busiest. Towns were the places where ideas were exchanged, where artists found encouragement and ordinary people found work and any hope of making a better living.

Cities were not large as we think of cities today. Many important ones had no more inhabitants than would fill an average football stadium. It was possible to walk across Florence in Italy in about 20 minutes, although you would have to twist and turn between the houses.

Most cities had walls to protect them from wolves, bandits and enemy armies. The walls also made it possible to keep a check on who, and what, was entering the city. Everything brought into the city was taxed at the gates. The gates were closed at night but there was usually an inn where travellers could stay if they arrived late.

The streets within the city were narrow. They made it easy to block the way of enemy soldiers who broke in, but they were also very unhygienic. Rubbish was thrown directly into the streets. It would then be eaten by pigs or would turn to a filthy slush that helped spread disease.

There was a strong sense of community. This centred round the church or cathedral that often towered above the town. The tightly packed houses huddled beneath it. Everyone knew what everyone else was doing. Life was about as private as it would be on a holiday site in high season.

Citizens had great local pride. There was no overall king of Italy. Each city had its own government, and people felt loyal to their own area, rather than to their country. Their rivals and enemies were not always from other countries, but often from rival cities. Even in France, where there was a King, the citizens of Lyons, for example,

Above: Siena was a busy Italian city during the Renaissance. This fresco shows the daily life of the citizens and countryfolk.

Left: The shoemaker was always busy. When people walked everywhere, in muddy streets and roads, boots wore out quickly.

Right: Ploughing, sowing and reaping. Townsfolk thought the country dangerous and unfriendly but relied on it for food.

thought of themselves as men of Lyons, rather than Frenchmen.

The wealth of each city depended on trade. Different towns became centres for different aspects of trade. Once a town or city became a famous centre, more merchants went there. This meant that more taxes could be raised and more business came the way of the local tradesmen.

Most townsfolk regarded the country with fear and suspicion.

For travellers who had to trudge or ride along muddy tracks, the country was certainly uncomfortable. It would often take several days to journey between two neighbouring towns. People usually travelled together in small groups or joined a convoy of merchants if they had to go through a particularly deserted area where there might be robbers or bands of roving mercenary soldiers.

Most people only fled to the country in time of plague to escape the crowded towns. Only a few saw it as a place of beauty, as you can see it portrayed in the background of some Renaissance paintings.

9

Power and Patronage

Because there was no king of Italy, political power lay with the rulers of the cities. These rulers are often referred to as princes of the Renaissance but very few had royal blood in them. Some came from aristocratic families. Others were from merchant families. It was simply the wealth and power that gave them the status of 'princes'.

Certain cities became very powerful and controlled large amounts of territory outside the city walls. This area often included smaller, less powerful cities. These became known as city states. They had their own rulers or governments, competed with each other in trade and industry and fought each other for greater power.

There were five main city states in Italy: Naples, Milan, Florence, Venice and the Papal States—the land controlled by the Pope. It was the rulers of these states, with their wealth, who became some of the greatest patrons of the Renaissance. It was also these rulers with their family ambitions and greed who caused the inter-city wars. The townsfolk preferred to get on with their work.

For a time, Milan was the strongest state, under its dukes, the Visconti family. One of the family, Gian Galeazzo, became so important that he married the daughter of King John II of France and one of his sisters married a son of King Edward III of England. After the Visconti, the Sforza family ruled Milan—first Francesco Sforza, a great mercenary captain, and then Ludovico Sforza, known as *Il Moro*, or the Moor, because of his dark face.

Florence and Venice were both republics; that is, states with an elected government, or *signory*. In fact, in Florence only about 3200 of the 100,000 inhabitants in 1495 were allowed to vote to elect members to the Signory. One family became the virtual princes of Florence for more than half of the 15th century. This was the Medici family.

No great family dominated in Venice, which tried to keep out of the continual inter-state fighting so

that it could concentrate on its overseas trade. It was ruled by the *Doge*, a man who was elected for life, and a Grand Council. There was also the Council of Ten which helped to keep public order in times of emergency. This council was dreaded because it was above the law. If it suspected someone of plotting against the state, it would have him killed.

The Popes were political leaders and patrons of the arts quite as much as they were leaders of the Church.

Left: Niccolò Macchiavelli, who believed that princes and rulers should assert their power.

Two of them were from the Medici family. Another was the father of the notoriously cruel Cesare Borgia who fought to increase family power.

Borgia was the model for a book, *The Prince* by Macchiavelli. Macchiavelli believed that rulers should stop at nothing, neither treason nor murder, to increase their power.

However, they did not always have the power to behave like Macchiavelli's prince. More often they had to rely on the friendly approach to keep the support of their people. Federigo da Montefeltro of Urbino, for instance, would go down to the market and chat with the workmen, doffing his cap to each one. People soon referred to things being 'as busy as Federigo's bonnet'.

There were other princes who were great patrons outside Italy. In England, Humphrey, Duke of Gloucester and younger brother of King Henry V, encouraged artists and writers. In France, the powerful Dukes of Burgundy led a very splendid court and Leonardo da Vinci actually died at the court of King Francis I.

Right: Federigo da Montefeltro, Duke of Urbino, was a learned patron and a soldier as well.

Above: Richly dressed English ambassadors are greeted at a Renaissance court in Venice. The painting is one of a series by Carpaccio.

Soldiers of Fortune

The knight in his armour had once been lord of the battlefield. Nothing could stop his charge and no common soldier could stand against him. But at the battles of Crécy and Agincourt Welsh longbows proved that the knight could be beaten. In later battles, the massed Swiss pikes, each more than five metres long and held by two men, formed a barrier through which no knight could easily pass. Even the ordinary foot-soldier, armed with a *halberd*—a pole with a hook and axe on the end—could drag a knight from his horse. Once down, the knight had difficulty getting up again. His armour was made of nearly 20 separate pieces and could weigh as much as 160 kilogrammes.

Warfare in Italy during the Renaissance became a very professional business. Princes were anxious to win more land and to conquer neighbouring cities to increase their wealth. However, the citizens themselves—the merchants and working people—were reluctant to leave their trades and join in the fighting. It was more profitable to hire an army to do the fighting for them. Armies of mercenary soldiers were led by captains, or *condottieri*—so called because they signed contracts, or *condotte*, to fight for a particular city for a certain length of time. They could even find themselves fighting against the city that had paid them the previous month. Often cities would pay a besieging army, that had come to lay siege, not to attack them. But sieges were rarely successful because city walls were too strong. Although cannon had been used at Crécy in the 14th century, firearms and cannon were still very primitive 100 years later. They could cause as much damage to the men who fired them as to the enemy!

The condottieri were among the greatest characters of the Renaissance. They often rivalled the princes they served in wealth and power.

Sir John Hawkwood, an Englishman, won great fame with his White Company, known for the brightness of its armour and its efficiency. He

Left: *The Battle of San Romano,* painted by Uccello. 15th-century knights clash in a fierce charge, with broken lances and bits of armour littering the ground. The battle continues in the distance.

Right: A portrait of the condottiere, Francesco Sforza, who ruled Milan for 16 years.

Below: A Renaissance painter's impression of the Battle of Pavia, fought between Francis I of France and Charles V of Spain. It was here that the true superiority of firearms over spears and swords was proved for the first time.

fought in turn for the Pope, the Visconti family of Milan and for Florence.

Muzio Sforza won the name *sforza,* or force, for his brave deeds but in the end he drowned when helping a page cross a stream just before a battle. His son, Francesco Sforza, carried on the family tradition and became one of the greatest of the condottieri. Francesco's wife, Bianca Maria Visconti, was as brave as he was. While he was away fighting a campaign, she herself led a band of soldiers to attack a rebellious town rather than send for her husband's help. With her beside him, Francesco ruled Milan for 16 years.

Bartolommeo Colleoni fought mostly for the Venetians. He became so famous that the artist Verrocchio made a magnificent statue of him that still stands in Venice. Erasmo da Narni known as *Gattamelata,* or the honeyed cat, also has a statue in his memory in Padua by the great sculptor Donatello.

The rich patron from Urbino, Federigo da Montefeltro, won money to pay for his splendid court and his horses by working for both Florence and Naples as a condottiere. One of the Medici family, too—Giovanni delle Bande Nere or Giovanni of the Black Company—was a condottiere. There is a story that one day he ordered his wife to throw their baby down from the balcony for him to catch in order, he said, to teach the baby fearlessness. Cesare Borgia was one of the few military leaders who did not use mercenaries but captained the armies of his father, the Pope.

Once again, it was the peasants who suffered most from inter-city warfare. The mercenaries trampled over their land, stealing whatever they wanted. An army of 30,000 or 40,000 soldiers might have three times as many camp followers, because they took their families with them as they travelled round the country in search of employment. When they were not in demand, they would separate into bands of looters that terrorized the neighbourhood.

The Medici of Florence

Of all the families that became powerful during the Renaissance, the Medici family was one of the most influential. In the 15th century they were the virtual rulers of Florence for three generations. During that time the city flourished and prospered.

The Medici family was immensely wealthy. Its members were merchants who traded in luxury goods from the East and they controlled a high proportion of the profitable market in cloth. They were also very successful bankers, with a string of banks throughout Europe and many influential clients—including Popes.

The family fortune was first established by Giovanni Medici and it was further increased by his son Cosimo. Cosimo was not just a good businessman. He was also a thoughtful man and a shrewd politician. As a young man he had studied and became interested in classical Greek works. These taught him that every citizen had a responsibility to contribute to society as well as benefit from it and, when his father died in 1429, Cosimo decided to follow a political career. In an age of violent rivalry between cities, Cosimo avoided war whenever possible. He preferred to negotiate and to use the power of his money. He was successful enough to guarantee Florence a long period of relative peace and security. Cosimo also allowed people to think and speak as they pleased—but he made a note of those who spoke against him.

Cosimo was one of the first great patrons of the Renaissance and took an interest in all the arts and sciences. Among the people he encouraged are the sculptors Ghiberti and Donatello, the architect Brunelleschi and the scholar Ficino. He had a great palace built in Florence which served as the main bank as well as the family home. It had a fortress-like ground floor with a massive door and barred windows to keep out enemies, but the upper storeys were very elegant. It was designed by the architect Michelozzo, who was also commissioned by Cosimo to design a library at the monastery of

Above: Lorenzo de Medici, the uncrowned 'prince' of Florence, was a patron of many great artists and a poet himself.

S. Giorgio Maggiore in Venice. Cosimo enjoyed encouraging an interest in books and learning (he allowed many well-educated men to borrow books from his own library) but this gift to the monastery was also a shrewd way of guaranteeing the political support of the Pope.

Cosimo controlled Florence for 30 years. When he died in 1464 he was succeeded by his son Piero. Piero had never enjoyed good health—he was known as Piero the Gouty—and he died after only five years. His 20-year-old son, Lorenzo, then became Florence's leading citizen. Lorenzo was not so interested in increasing the profits of banking. He preferred to spend much of the family fortune on the splendour of his court and on patronizing the artists,

FIORENZA

Above: The city of Florence in Renaissance times, surrounded by a defensive wall and with its domed cathedral in the centre.

Left and below: Lorenzo's brother, Giuliano, is dramatically murdered in Florence Cathedral. In the background friends help Lorenzo escape through a side door. Afterwards, there were riots in the street and several of the conspirators were hanged and thrown in the river.

Above and below: A medallion was struck by Lorenzo to commemorate the murder of his brother Giuliano.

architects and sculptors whose work made Florence such a beautiful city. Lorenzo himself had many talents. He enjoyed sports; he was a poet (who is still much admired today). He was also a successful statesman. His popularity and power aroused the jealousy of a rival Florentine family, the Pazzi. They conspired to assassinate Lorenzo and his brother Giuliano during High Mass in Florence Cathedral. Giuliano was killed but Lorenzo was only wounded. The citizens of Florence were outraged at this crime and rioting broke out. Many of the conspirators were dragged through the streets and thrown in the river in revenge.

The Medici family achieved great honour when Lorenzo's son, Giovanni, was made a cardinal at the age of 14. Giovanni later became Pope and took the name Leo. Like his father, Leo was an enthusiastic patron of the arts. In fact he took a great deal more interest in the arts and especially in the rebuilding of St Peter's in Rome, than he did in the church. Two years after he died in 1521, his cousin became Pope Clement VIII—the second Medici to be elected Pope. He was, however, politically weak and supported first Charles V and then Francis I in their rivalry.

Wealth and Trade

There was a clear distinction in the Dark Ages between the knights and the Church on one side and the poor people on the other. During the Renaissance a new social group emerged: the merchants. They became very wealthy and, because of their money, also became very powerful. 'A Florentine who is not a merchant,' wrote one citizen, 'who has not travelled through the world, seeing foreign nations and peoples, and then returned to Florence with some fortune, is a man who enjoys no esteem whatsoever.'

Meanwhile, the knights and the old aristocratic families often became less important and even quite poor. They were hangers-on at the great princely courts, trying desperately to keep up their social position.

Some of the more business-like resigned themselves to earning a living. They looked after their estates, acted as ambassadors or politicians, or even became paid government officials. To become a lawyer or a doctor was just about acceptable for a member of a well-to-do family. Younger sons could buy a career as a bishop or clergyman.

Some merchants found their wealth by trading silk and spices from the East. At first the merchants travelled in convoy overland to the eastern countries, but when the Turks captured Constantinople the land route was virtually cut off. The traders had to look for other routes and found the sea route around the Cape of Good Hope. They could also go by ship to Egypt, then overland to the Red Sea and then by ship to India.

The journey to India could take many months while that to the Far East might take more than a year. The ships were slow but could carry up to 1000 tonnes of cargo. They often returned from these trips with 20 times the value of the cargo they had taken out. However, the voyages were dangerous and many ships were lost, either by shipwreck or in fights with rival traders.

Other merchants made their money from the wool and cloth trades in

Above: Many merchants travelled great distances overland to bring their trade from the East before the sea-routes opened.

Europe. Wool was taken from England to Flanders where it was made into cloth that was sold at fairs to the Italian merchants. The high cost of transport over difficult roads made many products very expensive.

As well as importing exotic products, many merchants made their living by finding markets for goods that were manufactured in their own country.

The merchants met at great trading fairs in towns like Bruges and Lyons. There they bought and sold their wares and exchanged news. There was always an atmosphere of great festivity. It was the business and taxes provided by the merchants that brought prosperity to the cities along the great trading routes. Venice, Florence, Genoa, Milan, Lisbon, Bruges, Antwerp and Lyons are just a few that benefited.

There were always money exchangers and money lenders in the trading cities. They were disapproved of by the Church but, nevertheless, the handling of money became a trade in its own right. Many of the wealthiest families were bankers as well as merchants. In Florence it was the Medici family. In Augsburg it was the Fuggers.

Jakob Fugger, who was known as 'the Rich', had an international trading and banking organization. The headquarters were in a magnificent building known as the Golden Counting House. Agents wrote regular reports back to Augsburg, giving up-to-date information about the country they were in. Fugger newsletters often gave the merchants better information than any prince could obtain with his ambassadors or spies. The Fuggers even lent money to the Emperor Charles V. In return they were granted many trading privileges, which helped to increase their wealth.

The average merchant was a respectable character with a strong sense of family unity. The homes of the merchants were fairly simply furnished. Often the most elaborate item would be the *cassone*—a beautifully carved chest that a bride would take with her as part of her dowry. The superb decoration on these cassones was done by some of the best Renaissance artists.

Social rank and marriage was very important to both the aristocracy and the merchant classes. Sons could be married into wealthy families and so bring greater importance and fortune to their father.

Daughters, on the other hand, had to be provided with expensive dowries in order to attract suitable husbands. Families could not always afford dowries for all their daughters and so the younger ones often ended up in convents. In Florence there was a dowry bank into which a sum of money was paid when a girl was born. When she was 15 it was repaid with interest to provide a dowry. There was also a fund for girls with no dowry. A girl was considered ready for marriage at 12, but did not usually marry until 15 or 16. All unmarried girls were kept strictly at home and all women had to obey either their fathers or their husbands. Isabella d'Este of Ferrara was one of a very few women who were rich, powerful and clever enough to become patrons of art themselves.

Below: Ships unloading corn at the quayside. Goods brought by land and sea were sold at the great fairs and in town markets. At the bottom a merchant adds up what he has bought and sold.

17

Noble Entertainments

Whether they could afford to or not, nobles and merchants thought it most important to display their money. Some of the aristocracy still clung to the knightly pageantry of the past and organized elaborate tournaments. After the Turks had captured Constantinople in 1453 the Duke of Burgundy and Pope Pius II had started to plan a new Crusade. However, the Pope died just before the Crusade set off and the idea petered out. Instead, the knights displayed their out-of-date skills at tournaments held at the courts of Henry VIII of England, Francis I of France and the Holy Roman Emperor, Charles V. The tournament organized by Henry VIII for his meeting with Francis I was known as the Field of the Cloth of Gold, because it was such a rich and colourful spectacle. Another lavish display was the tournament known as the Tree of Gold. It was held in Bruges and organized by the Duke of Burgundy.

Armour and heraldry reached their most extravagant at these tournaments, and many people realized what a great waste of money —and life—they were. However, for the most part, the wealthy people were quite happy to attend, if only to see and be seen by neighbours and rivals.

Feasts were another good way to show off wealth. For example, when the Duke of Burgundy was planning his new Crusade he arranged the Feast of the Pheasant as a publicity stunt. There was a model church and a vast pie, both with live musicians inside. Other entertainments included singers, acrobats, an elephant and a falcon hunt inside the banqueting hall.

The wealthy also enjoyed spending their evenings playing music, singing and talking. Most kings and princes could play an instrument and some, such as Lorenzo de Medici and, later, Henry VIII, even composed their own songs. Many nobles kept a paid group of actors and musicians. Pope Leo X built up an excellent papal choir. In the French courts, the *cours d'amour* or courts of love, were known for poetry and the discussion of chivalry.

Chivalry was considered very important and one of the earliest books about good manners was written in 1528. This was *The Book of the Courtier* by Baldassare Castiglione. It outlined the perfect behaviour of *l'uomo universale*, the universal man, who should be athletic, artistic, loyal, well-read and not give offence.

Plays were popular. They were fairly serious, with moral or political stories, although there were some comedies based on the classical playwrights. The nobles would often join in, acting the main parts. People were quite happy to sit through four or five hours of a play, have an interval for food and then enjoy another two or three hours. The scenery was elaborate and there were also mechanical tricks, such as flashes of smoke, actors appearing on ropes and animals springing out of

Left: Music and poetry were very popular with the wealthy. This minstrel is playing a lute.

Right: A feast was always a good excuse for extravagance and entertainment among the rich. At this February feast a torch dance is accompanied by music.

ocks. These effects were considered so important that men as well-known as Leonardo da Vinci and Brunelleschi were sometimes commissioned to design them.

Although the wealthy enjoyed these intellectual pastimes, it was thought far more appropriate that they should participate in outdoor sports. These included archery, tennis, horseracing and, above all, falconry and hunting. Women enjoyed hawking as much as the men. One man wrote to Isabella D'Este complaining that his wife was much better at falconry than he was! Sometimes the women even went hunting for deer and wild boar. Princes would often take their entire courts hunting for several weeks at a time, and would entertain foreign princes while hunting. The hunting parties were enormous. There were no

Above: The princes and nobles often organized large hunting parties. This picture of the *Hunt in the Forest* was painted by Paolo Uccello when he was in Florence.

Right: Small birds and animals were hunted with falcons, trained by special falconers.

less than 300 horses in the great stables of Federigo da Montefeltro.

Hunting brought no pleasure to the peasants. There were laws forbidding them, on pain of cruel punishments, to kill the wild game themselves. The animals had to be kept for the princes. This meant that the peasants suffered twice. First the wild animals trampled and devoured their grain. Then the nobles rode through and ruined any crops that survived.

19

Fashion and Finery

Fashions during the Renaissance changed almost as fast as they do today, and foreign fashions were copied eagerly. Sometimes cloaks were short, sometimes long, sometimes parti-coloured stockings were much in style for men. Weddings and special occasions were an excuse to wear expensive silks and damask, ermine, velvet and taffeta.

Hats changed style with a speed that shocked people. One person complained: 'I know some women who have more heads than the devil.

Every day they put on some new headgear. I see some wearing them shaped like tripe, some like a pancake, some like a dish. If you could only see yourselves, you look like a lot of owls and hawks!' Laws were passed in many cities against such extravagance, but few people took much notice. Clothes were much too important as a mark of class distinction. In fact, a wealthy family would distribute smart clothes to all its servants so that the whole household would give a good impression when seen in public.

Above: The loose fitting sleeved shirt changed very little in design during the Renaissance.

Above: The tops of the hose, or stockings, were tied to the doublet, a jacket-like garment.

Left: A detail from Carpaccio's *Arrival of the Ambassadors*.

Above: Extravagantly styled and decorated head dresses were as popular with men as with women.

The strange fancy edging to the man's elaborate cap (far right) was known as dagging.

Above: The lady's chemise, worn under the dress, was a longer version of the man's shirt.

Above: The bodice of the dress fitted closely and fastened with laces down the front.

Right: An elegant sleeveless overdress completed the outfit.

Everyday Life

We read a lot about the princes and merchants of the Renaissance because of their wealth and power. In fact, they were only a small part of the population. The vast majority of townsfolk were ordinary labourers, shop-keepers, artisans and out-of-work poor. They represented 80 per cent of the people of Florence and, in the middle of the 15th century, there were 30,000 people in Florence too poor even to be taxed.

These citizens lived in close village-like communities within the town walls. They co-operated to help each other like an extended family, sharing duties such as fire-watch at night. Many people worked at home. If they had a shop, it was part of their two-room house. The working day was a long one, from sunrise to sunset with perhaps one hour altogether allowed for meal breaks. There were about 100 days free each year, including Sundays, Saints' days and in some towns, Saturday afternoons—but that was only to prepare for church on Saturday evening!

People worked hard in simple conditions. Even those who worked in the growing industries of shipbuilding, mining or metallurgy did not have to endure the grim factory conditions of the Industrial Revolution 300 years later. Larger industries often looked after their workers and took an interest in their health and welfare. They might even provide money for the family if a worker was ill or died. Some cities had special hospitals for the down-and-out and for foundlings.

Many workers were protected by the *guild* of their particular craft. This was rather like a modern trade union. The guilds controlled the quality and price of products and the number of people working in that trade. Often the guilds won a share in governing the city and could protect its members from rival craftsmen. Apprentices learnt their trade with a master and then became journeymen—people who travelled from town to town finding work. A journeyman could himself become a master if he passed certain strict guild exams. He had to produce a special piece of work which was known as his 'masterpiece'.

There were no guilds to protect the country folk. They lived a much harder life. Townspeople had a very poor opinion of them and seemed to believe that one peasant was worth only half a townsman. Unfortunately, in most of the countries of Europe, the huge majority of people were country peasants, scratching their existence from the land. They shared their home with their animals and the children and wives worked in the fields as hard as the men.

The soil was never dug deep enough to produce good crops and there were virtually no vegetables. Many people had only a wooden spade with which to dig and all the poor, in both town and country, lived largely on bread from the grain that the peasants grew. In that way, the peasants relied on the town for their market and the town relied on the country for its food. In between, the miller and the baker were two of the most important people in the community. The other important duty of the country was to provide wool to be made into cloth for clothing.

If there was famine or if soldiers took their crops, the poorest had only roots and nuts to eat or bread made partly from tree bark and grass seeds. In Spain the peasant remained very poor; in France and England some yeoman farmers were able to arrange a crop-sharing deal with their land-lord. It was only towards the very end of the Renaissance that improvements were made in agriculture and green vegetables such as beans, cabbages and cauliflower were developed. These made a tremendous difference to the health of everyone, rich and poor alike.

For the common people it was, on the whole, not a life to be envied. One person wrote at the time: 'The labouring poor is stripped of everything, downtrodden, oppressed, beaten, robbed, so that many are driven by want and hunger to leave their land.'

Above: Peasants in the country had to work on the land. *The Harvesters* was painted by Peter Breughel the Elder.

Left: Bread was an important part of the daily diet of the poor. Once the corn had been harvested, it was then threshed to separate the grain, then winnowed to clean the grain, then ground by the miller to produce the flour, and then it went to the baker to be baked into bread.

Sport and Spectacle

It may seem that the common people had little time for fun during the long, hard working week. They certainly could not afford oil for lamps or candles for light in the evenings. They did not have great feasts or go hunting—unless they could poach. They did not have rich clothes. But on Sundays and festivals they knew how to enjoy themselves.

Many festivals and pageants were organized by the rich but the ordinary people made the most of the occasion. They loved the excitement and the excuse to drink and sing. In Florence there were reckoned to be more than 60 taverns and 50 wine shops within about 10 minutes' walk of each other. Those that could afford it could drink a set amount of more than a litre of wine each day.

Mystery plays, or plays that told variations on Bible stories, had been popular since the Middle Ages. Everyone knew the stories by heart, but loved to see them again and again. The plays were usually performed on platforms in an open space in the town. Scenes of farce changed quickly to scenes of tragedy: the audience would first laugh, then

Right: A Florentine form of boxing known as *civettino;* they trod on each other's feet.

Far right: Half the city took part in this procession to celebrate a festival in Siena.

Below: A play is put on in the open at a village fête—from a painting by Peter Breughel.

cry and be always interested. The scenery was originally stark and symbolic. During the Renaissance, however, it became much more elaborate and realistic. For example, in a scene showing someone being burnt at the stake, a dummy might be filled with bones and the guts of animals which would fall out as the body burned.

Below: Football was played in a scrum of flying fists and legs. The ball was a pig's bladder.

Mystery plays were sometimes performed by travelling players, but often the local guilds would each take responsibility for one play in a series. They also organized scenes of pageants that celebrated important visitors and events. The pageants were made up of many little stages set up at street corners over a large area of the town. As the people walked from stage to stage, set scenes displayed a continuing story.

Processions usually took place on church festivals. Again, the guilds took part and every craft in the town would be represented by banners. In addition there would be pipers, drummers and trumpeters, bowmen, horsemen and foot-soldiers. There were carts, just like modern carnival floats. These might represent an entire ship, or a strange animal.

Even more exciting were the mock battles that were sometimes held.

The points of the weapons were covered but there were still plenty of bruises and broken heads. When these 'battles' were fought over the canal bridges in Venice half the people ended up in the water!

Other popular sports included wrestling and bear-baiting. Bear-baiting was very cruel. Dogs were set against a chained bear and several would be killed or maimed before the fight was stopped. The bear would then be led off to another show in the next town. It would quickly become a sorry-looking creature with torn ears, chunks of fur missing and masses of scars.

The poor enjoyed music as much as the rich did. Popular songs, or ballads, brought news of events in the outside world. They were spread from town to town by wandering singers and a good new ballad would soon be on everyone's lips.

25

Medicine and Disease

Both rich and poor were more used to seeing each other die than people are today. People died young and often suddenly. They died from disease, from malnutrition and from the injuries of war. Half the children born died before they were one year old. Many people did not live beyond 30 or 40. There were exceptions: Erasmus, the scholar, lived to about 70; Michelangelo died at 89 and the painter Titian lived well into his 80s.

There were plenty of so-called doctors but most knew nothing about the causes or cures for their patients' illnesses. Blood-letting was the most common remedy they tried. This was meant to let out 'bad' blood. A vein was cut with a knife or leeches were put against the skin to suck the blood. It was probably better—and safer—to rely on herbal books and housewives' remedies of drinks and lotions made from herbs. There were medicinal springs in the country in which the rich people sometimes bathed but no-one thought of swimming in the sea for their health.

In Italy, particularly, there were hospitals for the poor. The greatest good these did was to provide rest for the ill and to isolate those with

Above: Princes, priests and scholars are all led away to their fate by the skeletons of death in this illustration of a Dance of Death or *danse macabre*.

Below left: Victims of madness were sometimes operated on to remove the imaginary 'stones' from their heads which were supposed to cause the disease.

contagious diseases. Luther, the religious reformer, was most impressed by these hospitals when he visited Italy, although he did not like much else about the country.

Disease was easily spread in a city, where the houses were packed closely together and where rats came out at night to feed on the rubbish in the street. In England one of the causes of the spread of the dreaded 'sweating sickness' was believed to be the infected rush matting on the floors, soaked in the urine of the household dogs. Only the rich could afford soap which had been introduced to Italy in the 13th century. Some people wore a little piece of fur against the skin, which was supposed to draw the bugs away from the rest of the body.

The most terrible of all diseases was the Plague or Black Death. This first came to Europe from China in the 14th century. It sprang up again and again with equally awful effect for many generations, killing as much as one third of the population of many countries, and leaving whole villages empty. In five months in the summer of 1401, nearly 11,000 people died in Florence alone.

The task of burying the dead was so dangerous that criminals and vagabonds were used as gravediggers. They would often catch the disease themselves and, having caught it, would threaten to spread it in order to frighten or blackmail people.

Right: Medicines were sold by the apothecary, who mixed up the appropriate potions.

Below right: Bending over their books in bad light, scholars soon needed to buy spectacles.

Below: Some physicians used strange cures. This one prepares a lotion with vipers' bodies.

There was no cure for the Black Death. Doctors made a lot of money from false charms and fake remedies. Sweet-smelling herbs or foul-smelling rubbish were burnt in sickrooms to drive the Plague away. Victims ate pieces of paper on which prayers were written. Bells were rung to disturb disease-filled air. But after the first sign of a bluish-black abscess in the armpit or on the palm of the hand, inevitably there followed several days of agony and then death. City governments tried to cordon off areas of the city to stop the disease spreading. In Venice, an isolation hospital was established for all immigrants. The safest thing to do was to shut up shop and flee to the clean air of the country.

Worship and Scandal

In the Middle Ages all Christian people in Europe were members of one Church, which was ruled over by the Pope in Rome. Everyone recognized his authority and the authority of the priests. Often the priests were almost the only people in the town or village who could read or write and so people came to them for help and advice and the Church was the centre of community life.

The Church was still the centre of life during the Renaissance and people used the Church freely as a gathering place. Fear of death from the Plague made many people even more religious than before. They listened to sermons from famous preachers who said that the Plague was a punishment for their sins. But there were also many people who began to lose some of their fear and respect for the Church.

This change came about slowly. In many ways these people wanted a religion in which they could play a greater part instead of being ruled over by priests and the Pope. The Renaissance scholars had revived the idea of human dignity and their

teaching had encouraged people to question some of those things that they accepted blindly before.

One of the first questions that the more thoughtful people asked was whether it was right that the Pope should be so rich. For the popes had become just as interested in material wealth and possessions as the merchants and princes of the Renaissance. Popes Julius II and Leo X were both great patrons of the arts and spent huge amounts of money on commissioning buildings and works of art from artists.

Not surprisingly, many people thought this was scandalous. They also did not approve of some of the ways in which the Church got its money. One way was by the sale of relics. These were religious objects, such as pieces of saints' clothing or even their bodies, and bits of wood from the cross on which Christ was crucified. Pilgrims went on long journeys to visit places where these relics were kept and often paid a lot of money to buy them. Unfortunately many of the relics were false: the body of one saint, for example, might be

owned by one town and, apparently, have two or three heads, each claimed by two or three other towns. There were said to be enough pieces of Christ's cross around to build an entire ship.

Another scandal was the way in which the Church raised money by selling indulgences or pardons for sins that people had committed or were about to commit. The Church agent, or *pardoner*, went round the towns selling slips of paper bearing pardons from the Pope.

It was one of these agents, John Tetzel, who provoked Martin Luther into quarrelling with the Pope.

Tetzel urged people to buy pardons to save their souls, but in fact he was raising money for the rebuilding of St Peter's in Rome. Like others before him, Luther felt that the Church should not exploit people in this way. Also he did not think that a Pope in Italy should have power over his own German people and other foreign nationalities. Luther's desire for reform in the Church led to the movement called the Reformation. The Protestants, or those who protested against the Pope's authority, began fighting with the Catholics, who still accepted the authority of the Pope.

In some ways the Church helped the Renaissance. Michelangelo and Raphael did some of their best work for the Pope. And the great Church Councils that met occasionally brought people together from all over Europe and helped to spread the ideas and the new learning of the Renaissance. In fact, the scandals of the Church probably only worried a few thinking people. Throughout the Renaissance there was a great deal of faith in religion and discussion about it. This faith was perhaps best summed up in the *Imitation of Christ* by Thomas à Kempis, which was a sort of 15th-century guide to the religious life and has been an inspiration to many people ever since.

Left: This painting of the election of Pope Pius II shows the pageantry of the Church.

Top left: Martin Luther, whose quarrel with the Pope sparked off the Reformation.

Above: Michelangelo painted his famous *Creation of Adam* for the Pope's Sistine Chapel in Rome.

Top right: A Renaissance version of the popular theme of Christ and John the Baptist by Raphael.

Learning from the Past

PROHEMIVM LIBRI terhi.

Exhortatio ad bellum contra barbaros.

MARSILIVS fici
nus florentinus Mathie
felicissimo pannoniae re
gi i pace securitatem i
bello uictoriam inuicto
ria gloriam sempiternam uaticinatur.

PLATO NOSTER philosophorum
pater rex foelicissime Xenocratem Dionez
dilectos dyscipulos suos uiros quidem sanc
tos, sed paulo seueriores tristioresqz q decere
phos uideretur, saepe monere solebat ut gra
tys sacra diligentissime facerent, quo gratio
siores iucundioresqz redderentur. Qd autez
Platoni nro quondam erga dyscipulos duos
agendum fuit, idem in nunc erga geminos

Above: This page from a book by Marsilio Ficino shows a high standard of illumination in the opening letter and the margins.

Right: Marsilio Ficino is standing on the left in this painting of four humanist scholars by Ghirlandaio.

The greatest scholars and teachers of the Renaissance were known as the humanists. Their ideas provided the inspiration for much of the exciting thought and art of the time. Their name *humanist* came from the Latin word *humanitas* which means the belief in the value of every individual.

The humanists were very enthusiastic about the discovery and translation of old books, especially Greek and Latin books, because of the ideas there. They were most interested in the fact that many authors in Roman times had written about the pride and interest that man took in life. Although the Greeks and Romans believed in gods, they also believed that man had a great deal of independent control over his own life.

During the Middle Ages life had been dangerous and insecure because there were no powerful kings to keep the peace. People lost confidence in themselves and took very little interest in ideas outside the Church.

When the cities and the growth of trade gave people greater security, scholars once again had time to think about the ideas in the old books that they had rediscovered. They taught that man should have pride in his independent mind and the miracle of himself and life around him. Many believed that a greater enjoyment and understanding of the beauty of life would help people to have a greater enjoyment and belief in God. It was this link between man and God

hat made the ideas of the humanists acceptable to so many people.

It was also tremendously exciting for writers and artists who began to describe and portray the world accurately for the first time for years. Artists began to paint the human body in a much more lifelike way and even began to paint naked bodies. People took new interest in all sorts of ideas. They asked questions that no one had thought of asking for centuries and they tried to answer them by their own observations.

One of the most famous humanists was Marsilio Ficino, who was brought up by Cosimo de Medici and taught Cosimo's son, Lorenzo. He was a small, melancholy man, who was interested in a tremendous number of things, including playing the lyre—a sort of Greek harp. Another humanist was Lorenzo Valla, who insisted on accurate translations of old books because inaccurate translations led to misunderstandings. He never accepted what others said without studying the subject himself: 'I prefer to see with my own eyes,' he said, 'rather than with the eyes of others.'

The humanists' ideas spread all over Europe. They were great teachers and encouraged the building of schools. The scholar and humanist Erasmus spent most of his life travelling around Europe, teaching many of the kings, princes and bishops of his time. Like his friend Thomas More in England, he

Top: Scholars studying astronomy charted the routes of the planets with this instrument called an armillary sphere.

Above: The Renaissance scholars were greatly influenced by the books of ancient Greece, including those of the mathematician Pythagoras, portrayed here teaching arithmetic.

wanted to make many peaceful changes in society. Thomas More wrote *Utopia* as a picture of his ideal state. Many princes encouraged humanists to teach their children and some of the lessons they taught survived in schools for centuries.

In England boys were often sent off to other people's houses for their education. In Florence there were primary and high schools. A merchant might send his son to the *abacus*, a course in simple mathematics that would help him become a useful accountant. Children learnt mostly by heart, though some would have a hornbook or slate which could be wiped clean after each lesson and was handed down from brother to brother. Girls were rarely sent to schools but might have received a little education at home.

Standards of teaching varied, too. In some universities, lecturers were forced to make their lessons interesting because they were fined if they did not have about six students in their class. In Florence it was possible to get in to university after a grammar school education. At Padua students might be in their 20s or 30s and be more interested in drinking, singing and fighting.

The Printed Word

The spread of printing in the middle of the 15th century had an effect as dramatic as the invention of radio and television in this century. Try to imagine a world with no radio and no television; then try to imagine a world with scarcely any books. Before the age of printing, all books had to be copied out by hand. If you wanted a book and could afford it, first you had to find a copy, then you had to find someone to copy it. You might have to wait many months for the work to be done. In the end, every book was a little different and more and more mistakes would occur each time a book was copied. This made life very hard for humanist and church scholars, who had no standard text which they could all discuss.

For a long time, the Chinese had used carved wooden blocks to print from, but a whole new block had to be carved for each page. Woodblock illustrations and playing cards were very popular in Europe during the Renaissance. The Chinese also used individual letters made of wood or baked clay which could be made in quantities and changed around to form any word. But it was not until Gutenberg invented a satisfactory method of making these movable letters out of metal that printed books really became possible. The metal type could be made quickly in moulds and used over and over again. At the same time the expensive vellum and parchment of the past was given up. Instead, cheap linen rags were boiled to a pulp, strained through a sieve and left to dry and form sheets of paper strong enough to last for centuries. Paper was well established in Western Europe by the second half of the 14th century. It almost superseded vellum during the 15th century.

Gutenberg's one great work was the 42-line Bible (it had 42 lines on each page), which was finished in 1456. But as he was a bad businessman and became involved in endless lawsuits over the patent of his press he died a poor man. Nine years later, in 1465, printing reached Italy and the first

two books printed there were a Latin grammar and a book by Cicero, the Roman orator. In another nine years William Caxton had printed the first book in English at Bruges, a history of Troy, and four years later, in 1478, printed an edition of Chaucer's *Canterbury Tales* at his own sign of the Red Pale at Westminster, London.

The most famous publishing house in Venice was the Aldine Press, founded by Aldus Manutius. It was this printing house that invented the graceful type-face called *italic*. But there was stiff competition between printers: by the end of the 15th century there were 150 printers in Venice alone and more than 200 different editions of Cicero's works had been printed. Early editions of books consisted only of about 100-250 copies each but by the end of the century there were editions of about 1000 copies. It was about then that the first printed book catalogue appeared, with prices.

When large numbers of copies of a single book or pamphlet could be

Above: A scribe at his desk. Books had to be hand-copied before printing was invented.

Right: A page from Gutenberg's printed 42-line Bible.

Right: There were several stages in book printing. First the letters were moulded, then the compositor (left) arranged them in trays to make up words and lines. The trays were then inked (centre) and put in the press.

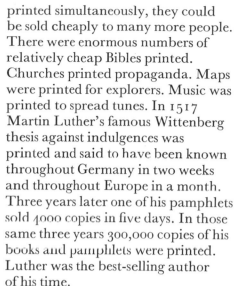

printed simultaneously, they could be sold cheaply to many more people. There were enormous numbers of relatively cheap Bibles printed. Churches printed propaganda. Maps were printed for explorers. Music was printed to spread tunes. In 1517 Martin Luther's famous Wittenberg thesis against indulgences was printed and said to have been known throughout Germany in two weeks and throughout Europe in a month. Three years later one of his pamphlets sold 4000 copies in five days. In those same three years 300,000 copies of his books and pamphlets were printed. Luther was the best-selling author of his time.

At first most of the books were in Latin but soon books were increasingly printed in the *vernacular*, the language spoken by the people of each country. Luther wrote in German; Caxton printed the *Canterbury Tales* in English. Popular books were soon translated into other languages. The highly successful *Ship of Fools* by Sebastian Brant of Strasbourg—a satire on the follies of mankind with exciting woodcut illustrations—was twice translated into English within a period of 15 years.

Above: The device used by William Caxton, who printed the first book in English.

New Horizons

The burst of interest in books greatly encouraged people's curiosity about the world about them. They re-read the ancient Greek and Roman geography books of Strabo and Ptolemy; they carefully read descriptions of the travels of Arab explorers like Masudi and Ibn Battuta. They were fascinated by the *Travels* of Marco Polo and, for light relief, they enjoyed the fanciful tales of Sir John Mandeville which told of monsters and imaginary lands.

On a more practical level, they were keen to find trade routes to the East. The capture of Constantinople by the Turks virtually closed the normal overland routes. New ones were hard to find because the early Renaissance view of the world was limited and badly distorted. They did not know of the existence of America,

although Norse explorers had probably been there long before, and they did not believe they could sail round Africa into the Indian Ocean.

At the beginning of the 15th century, the Portuguese took the first steps of exploration down the African coast. They had won a foothold from the Moors in north-west Africa and Prince Henry the Navigator set up a centre for navigation there at the beginning of the 15th century. Ships used a simple compass for navigation. Sailors estimated their latitude by measuring the angle of the Pole Star or sun above the horizon with a quadrant or astrolabe. They also used a lead, which was swung down into the water to gauge the depth.

The ships themselves were small but sturdy and fully rigged with sails. The old, heavy ships with oarsmen

would have been too laden and too slow for long expeditions. The *caravel* was one of the most useful ships. It weighed between 50 and 100 tonnes and was usually less than 30 metres long. A modern supertanker is five or ten thousand times heavier.

Life on board for the 40 or 50 men was tough and wet. Not many men chose to be sailors. Some of Columbus' crew were criminals because he, at the last minute, was unable to raise a full crew. They slept on deck or with the stores or the ballast—gravel or sand which helped to stabilize the ship. They had no hammocks until they learnt about them from the American Indians.

Columbus was sure that he could reach the East by travelling west, around the world. He went with three ships and the journey took him

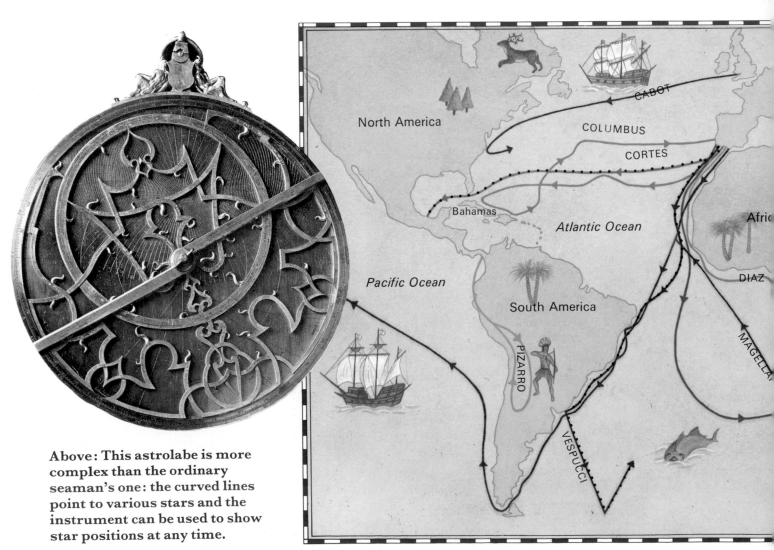

Above: This astrolabe is more complex than the ordinary seaman's one: the curved lines point to various stars and the instrument can be used to show star positions at any time.

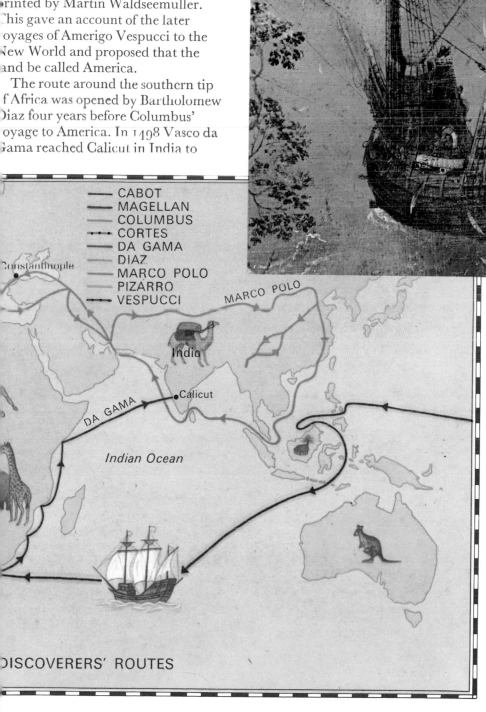

month, in 1492. He stepped ashore
on one of the islands in the Bahamas
wearing a dark velvet suit and violet
silk stockings and bearing a letter to
the Great Khan of China. He was
extremely surprised to be met by
naked savages who only wanted
bangles. Although he made three
more expeditions, he never realized
that he had discovered a new
continent. A year after his death
1000 copies of a World Map were
printed by Martin Waldseemuller.
This gave an account of the later
voyages of Amerigo Vespucci to the
New World and proposed that the
land be called America.

The route around the southern tip
of Africa was opened by Bartholomew
Diaz four years before Columbus'
voyage to America. In 1498 Vasco da
Gama reached Calicut in India to

CABOT
MAGELLAN
COLUMBUS
CORTES
DA GAMA
DIAZ
MARCO POLO
PIZARRO
VESPUCCI

Constantinople

MARCO POLO

India

Calicut

DA GAMA

Indian Ocean

DISCOVERERS' ROUTES

**Above: A two-masted sailing ship
of about 1550, very much like the
ships of the early explorers.**

begin a long history of sea voyages
and trade round the Cape of Good
Hope. The year before, John Cabot
was sent by Henry VII of England
to explore the coastline of North
America. The first expedition to sail
round the world more than 20 years
later was led by Magellan. Magellan
himself was killed on the voyage and
only one of the ships reached home.

Everyone understood the
discoveries to the East: they meant
more trade. But the discovery to the
West of a whole new continent was
something extraordinary. It was not
until Cortés and Pizarro brought back
tales of gold among the Aztecs and
Incas and the first great silver mines
were discovered in the middle of the
16th century that people fully began to
appreciate the material value of the
New World.

The Search for Truth

The Renaissance had very few scientists, as we think of them—that is, men who specialize in chemistry, physics, zoology, biology and so on. Science was the Roman word for knowledge and the Renaissance scholars thought of science in the same way. It meant any kind of knowledge. A scientist was someone who read old books or did his own practical experiments to find out more about the world around him. Gradually, many scientists became less interested in the old books and more interested in trying to find things out for themselves. 'Burn up your books,' advised one Renaissance scientist, 'Watch and experiment without ceasing.'

The most revolutionary scientific theory of the time was in astrology, the study of the stars. Nicolaus Copernicus watched the planets and stars for over 30 years and carefully

Above: This picture shows a medieval concept of a sphere surrounding a flat earth and mechanics that moved the stars.

Left: Leonardo da Vinci was a scientist as well as an artist. He drew this detailed picture of a baby in the womb.

re-read many ancient Greek and Arab books. His conclusion was that the Earth was not at the centre of the Universe, but that the Earth went round the sun. This was most upsetting because, throughout the Middle Ages and for a great deal of the Renaissance, it had been generally agreed that the sun went round the Earth. People believed that the Earth was in the middle of a perfectly symmetrical universe, with God and the Church at the very centre. Copernicus' theory came towards the end of the Renaissance, in the middle of the 16th century, and spoilt this neat arrangement. It also angered the Church because it upset their central authority. Seventy years after his death and the publication of his famous book, *On the Revolutions*

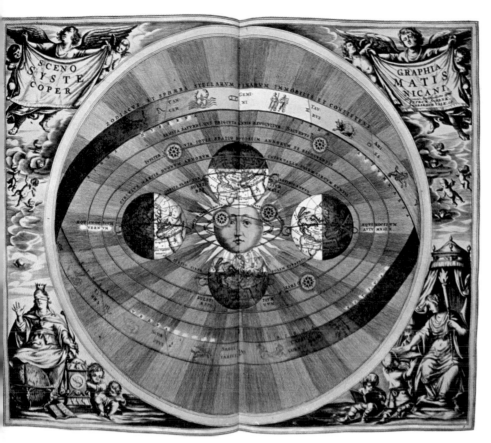

Above: Copernicus contradicted common beliefs when he said that the Earth went round the sun, as this picture illustrates.

Below: The title page of Vesalius' book on the human body, which has many careful drawings of muscles and veins.

shipbuilding and metallurgy all became very important. Watermills were used more and more to pump out mines and to drive machinery in the mills themselves. Railroads were laid in many mines, to make it easier to run the horse-drawn carts. Firearms improved slowly but were still dangerously likely to explode. Clocks became increasingly popular and by 1500 most European towns had a public clock; the coiled spring was invented at that time, which made it possible to make pocket watches, too.

But for most of the Renaissance, even princes were happy to cling to the past. They relied on astrologers to warn them about the future and many believed that the future could be controlled by magic spells. The search for the secret of turning ordinary metal into gold fascinated everyone who wanted to get rich quickly. Alchemists tried every kind

of the *Celestial Spheres*, the Church named him as a heretic.

Many years later, when Galileo published descriptions of stars and planets seen through his telescope and proved what Copernicus had said, he too was accused of heresy and threatened with torture if he did not deny what he wrote. In the meantime another astronomer, Johannes Kepler, had upset the idea of a perfect world even more by claiming that the Earth did not orbit the sun in a circle but in an ellipse or oval.

The first Renaissance man to publish a thorough study of the human body was Andreas Vesalius, who started work in Paris and spent most of his life in Italy. When only 29, he produced a magnificent work called *The Seven Books on the Structure of the Human Body*. It contained more than 270 beautiful woodcut illustrations showing the body's bones, muscles, veins and heart. His book was another sign of the growing curiosity about life. It was published in the same year in which Copernicus' book appeared.

There were several advances made in industry and technology during the Renaissance. Printing, mining,

Above: The Nuremburg Egg dates from about 1500 and is one of the earliest pocket watches. It has its own silver case and key.

of recipe, most of which were as extraordinary and useless as a witch's brew, and confidence tricksters made fortunes by selling what they swore was the 'real' secret. But, during their hopeless efforts to turn the Earth's minerals into gold they did learn a great deal about these minerals. Their knowledge proved useful to the scientists of a later age.

Leonardo da Vinci

The most brilliant scientist of the Renaissance was also one of its greatest artists. Leonardo's fame does not rest just on his paintings, of which only about 12 survive, but on his drawings and notebooks and the reputation for genius that he had even in his lifetime.

Leonardo's notebooks are filled with sketches of fossils, plants, skeletons, muscles, embryos and eye structures. There are irrigation schemes, lathes, pumps, cranes, diving helmets, steam engines and notes on the strength of building materials. There is an aeroplane, a helicopter, a military tank and a machine gun. There are 5000 pages in all, with drawings and notes on an extraordinary range of subjects. Many of his machines would never have worked in practice but the ideas were often far more advanced and imaginative than most people could understand.

Leonardo was born in the village of Vinci, near Florence, in 1452. He had almost no education. One of the reasons he was such a good scientist was that he had to find out everything for himself, although he later read a good deal. He lived in Florence while Lorenzo de Medici governed the city and learnt the skills of painting in the studio of the artist Verrocchio.

He painted one of the angels in *The*

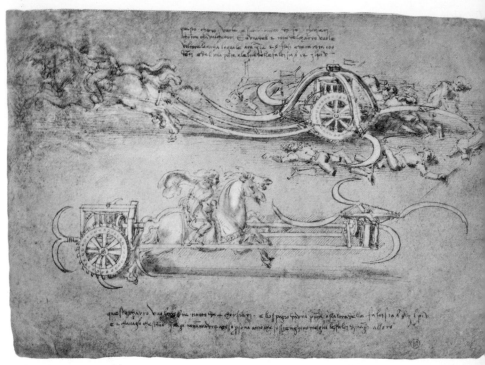

Above: A self-portrait of the great Leonardo da Vinci. He lived until he was 67 but this picture makes him look older.

Top: Leonardo designed some very frightening war machines but these scythe-like chariots were never actually made.

Above: Leonardo's drawing of a perfectly proportioned man was inspired by the ancient Roman architect Vitruvius.

Baptism of Christ by Verrocchio and it is said that when Verrocchio saw how much better than his own figures was the one done by Leonardo he decided to give up painting. One of the greatest paintings from those early days in the city of Florence was the *Adoration of the Magi*, which Leonardo never finished. He became notoriously unreliable and was far more interested in satisfying his own curiosity than satisfying his patrons.

He spent 16 years working in Milan on a statue of Francesco Sforza, the father of his patron Ludovico Sforza, but he never completed the bronze casting. The clay model was eventually used for archery practice by the French bowmen who invaded Milan. No statue by Leonardo survives. After working in Florence again and, briefly, for Pope Leo X in Rome, he died working at the French court of Francis I.

It was in Milan that Leonardo painted *The Last Supper*. This shows his skill in painting characters full of life and energy. Unfortunately he used oil paints, a new technique at the time that he had not completely mastered. The painting began to decay even in his own lifetime. His famous *Mona Lisa*, or *La Gioconda*, has survived much better. Leonardo, it is said, provided men to sing to her and buffoons to amuse her to make her smile, because he did not like the usual melancholy portraits. There are very subtle tones of colour and very delicate changes between light and shade in the picture which make her face look extremely lifelike. The background scenery in this and other paintings is typical of Leonardo's interest in landscape and detail. He believed that all forms of knowledge were essential to the artist, even mathematics, and he made careful calculations on perspective in paintings.

Leonardo probably thought of himself as much an engineer as an artist. Most of his skill, however, went only into making clever devices for pageants and parades. He made a mechanical lion for the King of France. This took a few steps forward and then opened its breast to show a whole mass of lilies—a French symbol. His mind flitted from subject to subject and there was never enough time to finish the really important things. He scribbled impatiently over a page of his notebooks: 'Tell me if anything at all was done.' It usually was not and it is only recently that his notebooks have been studied closely.

Above: The quiet smile of the *Mona Lisa* (*La Gioconda*), perhaps Leonardo's most famous and well-loved painting.

Right: Leonardo's *Lady with an Ermine*. The ermine is both a pet and a pun on the lady's surname.

New Attitudes to Artists

It was during the Renaissance that artists began to be recognized as individuals rather than as good working craftsmen. Until then there was not even a guild of painters. They belonged instead to the guild of apothecaries because of the way they mixed their paints rather than how they used them. Sculptors belonged to the guild of stonemasons and bricklayers. The guilds fixed the price for a job and the subject matter and materials were ordered by the employer. He expected the work to be done exactly as he wanted, so there was very little scope for the craftsman to experiment with his own ideas.

However, with the encouragement of rich patrons like the Medici, certain artists were able to escape from the steady employment of the guild workshops. This gave them the chance to develop their own styles.

It took time for people to appreciate the difference between a craftsman and an artist. At first, even the great patron Cosimo de Medici had found it hard to accept. There is a story that he persuaded the sculptor Donatello to wear a uniform because he did not like his ordinary clothes. After only a few days, Donatello complained that it was undignified and refused. On another occasion, Donatello broke a head that he had

sculpted, in fury at being offered what he considered to be far too low a price by the merchant who ordered it.

The idea of the special artistic temperament began to spread. Isabella d'Este, waiting impatiently for a painting by Giovanni Bellini, was warned 'to get used to the fantasy of what he is doing, as he does not like too fixed limitations to be placed on his style'. When the monastery for which Leonardo da Vinci was painting *The Last Supper* complained that he seemed to spend more time looking at the painting than getting on with the work, Leonardo explained with irritation that a genius was working just as hard when he was thinking as when he was actually painting.

But many people still found it hard to accept the value of the artist. Michelangelo's family, which was fairly respectable, was horrified when he said he wanted to be a sculptor. Lorenzo de Medici himself had to persuade them that their son was going to be something more worthy than a stone-cutter.

In time, artists commanded the respect and friendship of princes and popes. Titian, for example, was knighted by Charles V for painting his portrait. Princes began to send artists abroad to show off their skills

and to spread the fame of the prince's court. Artists found that they could move freely from country to country, finding a welcome from patrons everywhere. Leonardo and the goldsmith Benvenuto Cellini both worked in France as well as Italy. Other Italian artists visited Moscow, Spain, Germany, the Netherlands and England. Dürer travelled from Germany to Italy where he found that he was even more popular than at home.

The fact that Dürer signed his drawings showed that the artist was considered as important as the work of art. There was much interest in the artists as people. A famous book, Vasari's *Lives of the Artists*, was written while Michelangelo was still alive. Cellini wrote his own life story and the book is bursting with confidence and self-congratulation.

Their improved status allowed artists to experiment with new techniques and styles. There was more interest in the human body, in perspective and in landscape. They experimented with the use of oil paints instead of tempera, in which the colours had been mixed with egg-yolk. The Venetian artists used layers of paint and made the colours glow through. Leonardo used a technique of shading called *sfumato*.

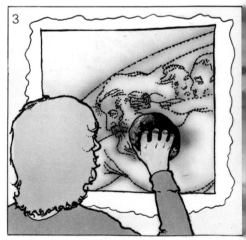

Above: Fresco painters used different methods. Here is a typical one. First, a full size outline, or cartoon, of the fresco was made on large sheets of paper (1). **This was cut into squares, each representing one day's work. Holes were pricked along the outline. The whole wall was plastered roughly** (2) **and** left to dry. **Each day a small area of wall was plastered smoothly and a section of the cartoon was placed against it** (3). **A bag containing charcoal powder was**

Frescoes, or pictures which were
painted on to wet plaster, remained
popular. Michelangelo's paintings in
the Sistine Chapel are done in fresco
and they remain fresh and bright to
this day.

The reputation of the craftsman
naturally suffered as the best artists
became a select group. More and
more, the skilled craftsmen were
hired simply to do the hard labour.
The artists became more and more
favoured. It was said that 'in Italy
one does not care for the renown of
great princes; it's a painter only
that they call divine'.

Right: Michelangelo had to work
on a scaffold, lying flat on his back
close to the ceiling for his vast
fresco in the Sistine Chapel.

rubbed over the pricked cartoon.
This left a dotted outline on
the fresh plaster. The dots were
joined up and the shading was
put in with ochre colour (4).

The paints were mixed with water
in goblets (5). They had to be
prepared in advance each day.
The range of colours was limited.
Fine brushes were made with

bristles in quills. Each section
was completed before the plaster
dried (6). The artist always
started at the top of the wall
and worked downwards.

The Painters of Italy

One of the great Renaissance Popes, Pius II, explained that 'Pictures produced 200 years ago were not refined by any art but after Giotto the hands of the painters were raised once more.' What he meant by unrefined pictures were the flat, two-dimensional paintings of the Middle Ages, copied from the art of Byzantium. There was no attempt to show depth, movement or the form of the human body.

Giotto was the first to try to give shape to the body and to give some three-dimensional effect to his pictures. His famous frescoes in Assisi, Florence and Padua still had religious subjects but were far more lifelike than earlier paintings. There is a story that he was discovered by the artist Cimabue when, as a boy, Giotto was drawing his father's sheep on a flat stone. Later, he painted a fly on the face of a figure that Cimabue was drawing. The fly was so lifelike that Cimabue tried to brush it away. When asked to send a sample of his work to Pope Benedict IX to try for a job in Rome, Giotto simply drew a perfect circle with his brush—and got the job.

His interest in the human body was carried on by the artist Masaccio, a Florentine who died when he was only 27. The calm and simple paintings of the humble monk Fra Angelico and the famous *Annunciation* of Fra Filippo Lippi followed Masaccio in using light and shade to give an idea of three-dimensional perspective. The use of light to add drama to a picture appears also in the paintings of Piero della Francesca.

Perspective was one of the great artistic discoveries of the Renaissance. Leon Battista Alberti wrote an essay about painting and explained how important perspective was to an artist. He called it 'a subject never before treated'. More than almost any other artist, Paolo Uccello was fascinated by using perspective, as you can see in the *Battle of San Romano*. He also loved to paint landscape, animals and birds.

Each painter contributed some-

Top: Giotto was one of the first Renaissance painters. His figures took on real shape.

Above: In this *Annunciation*, Fra Angelico uses light and shade to give depth.

thing fresh and exciting to the Renaissance. Botticelli loved mythological subjects and the decorative detail and colour that were characteristic of some of the northern Gothic painters. Flowers brighten the *Birth of Venus*. In Florence, artists experimented with the patterns of lines in their paintings, but in Venice the emphasis was on colour. The climate spoiled wall-paintings done in fresco, so artists preferred to use oils on canvas. From Venice came the dramatic lighting of Tintoretto's pictures and the rich energetic pictures by Titian.

The massive, powerful bodies in Michelangelo's paintings are very well known, although he preferred sculpture to painting. The ceiling that he painted in the Sistine Chapel, Rome, took him four and a half years to do. At first he had assistants to help him but he was dissatisfied with their work and he completed the whole thing himself. Most of the time

Above: *The Birth of Venus* by Botticelli shows the artist's love of colour and use of detailed decoration.

he lay on his back so close to the ceiling that he could hardly see what he was doing.

Raphael also painted some famous frescoes which are still in Rome and he designed the tapestries which were meant for the other walls in the Sistine Chapel. The tapestries were sent to Brussels to be woven. Raphael was a very popular painter and the beautiful Madonnas that he painted in Florence are richly coloured and yet appear soft and gentle.

Leonardo thought that Giotto and Masaccio were the only painters worth imitating. In his paintings, many of the special Renaissance interests are fulfilled—three-dimensional depth, background detail, living portraits and clever use of light and shade.

Northern European Painters

The painters in northern Europe were, surprisingly, only slightly influenced by their contemporaries in the south. They had their own traditions and they developed them in their own way. They did not have the same feeling for Greece and Rome that the Italians had. This made their paintings less majestic and classical, more down-to-earth, more realistic and, sometimes, more cheerful.

One of the first great northern painters was Jan van Eyck, who was neither very good at perspective nor at anatomy but painted superb detail and developed the use of oil painting. His famous *Marriage Portrait of Giovanni Arnolfini* shows how good he was at painting a realistic scene—his

own reflection appears in a mirror hanging behind the couple. The use of oil instead of egg-yolk to bind his powdered colours enabled him to work the colours smoothly into each other as he painted, because the oil dried more slowly than the egg. He could also produce glossy colours applied in thin layers.

Dürer had the same interest in detail but was a far better draughtsman than Jan van Eyck and could draw people, animals and plants perfectly. Like Leonardo, he was fascinated by mathematics and believed geometry to be 'the right foundation of all painting'. He even wrote an essay on the design of military fortifications. Brought up in Nuremberg, he visited Italy twice and painted some beautiful water colours of the country. He was mostly interested in graphic work, such as line drawings, woodcuts and

engravings. Altogether he completed about 2000 drawings, 250 woodcuts and over 100 engravings.

The lively, cheerful scenes of Peter Breughel the Elder's paintings show the realism of northern painting at its most down-to-earth. He shows characters with simple, often ugly faces, and distorted bodies having fun, teasing and sometimes hurting each other. These paintings are satires, bringing out the good and bad points of the characters in an extreme way, despite the realism of the landscape.

Breughel was influenced to some extent by one of the strangest of the northern painters, Hieronymous Bosch. His figures are tormented by weird and terrifying beasts and suffer cruel tortures on their way from the

Below: Jan van Eyck's *Marriage Portrait* is packed with detail even in the dog's hair.

Below: This beautifully detailed and realistic picture of a hare was painted by Dürer.

Above: The strange figures and wild imagination of Bosch are often very frightening.

Below: Holbein's *Ambassadors*. The skull becomes clearer when viewed from an angle.

Garden of Eden to Hell. These pictures show how much the northern mind was still concerned with religion and the fear of damnation that had frightened people of the Middle Ages.

Grunewald, too, painted symbolic and religious pictures. His dramatic *Crucifixion* on the Isenheim alterpiece shows more interest in the emotional agony of Christ than in a perfectly shaped human form. Albrecht Altdorfer adds delightfully romantic landscapes to many of his paintings. The northern sense of detail is shown even in the miniatures of the French painter Jean Fouquet.

The German artist Hans Holbein the Younger fled to England at the Reformation and became court painter to Henry VIII. The people in his famous portraits appear to be much more confident than many of the characters in northern pictures. One of the noticeable differences between north and south is that Italian portraits show people who have a confidence and control that the northerners lack. The Italians painted popes, princes and merchants, who *were* confident, of course. Northern artists often painted peasants and middle-class people who were not in such control of their own fate. That is, perhaps, what makes them more human.

Sculpture in the Round

For many hundreds of years before the Renaissance the only kind of sculpture there had been was called *relief*. A relief was a figure only half cut out of a block of stone. It was usually quite shallow, not very lifelike and there was little attempt to create any kind of realistic scene around the figure.

There were no real sculptors either. The work was done by skilful stonemasons who were more used to cutting great blocks of stone for building than carving figures of saints for decoration. You can see these kinds of relief still, particularly on the walls of some of the great medieval cathedrals. Some modern business buildings also have relief sculptures on their walls for decoration.

In time, the lessons about background detail and perspective, which had been learnt in painting by Giotto and the early Renaissance artists, began to be used in sculpture. You can see how the reliefs became more lifelike in the famous doors that Lorenzo Ghiberti designed for the Baptistry in Florence. The city held a competition in 1401 to decide who should make the great pair of bronze doors. Ghiberti won the competition against the architect Brunelleschi and many others. He took 21 years to complete the 10 New Testament scenes on each door. The backgrounds of the scenes contain much detail of architecture and landscape and the use of perspective gives the reliefs a feeling of depth. The Florentines were so delighted that they ordered another pair of doors from Ghiberti. Michelangelo said that the second pair were worthy to be called the Gates of Paradise and they are still known as that even today.

The next step in reviving the sculpture of Greece and Rome was the figure that stood on its own. The free-standing statue was another example of the humanist attitude and the way in which the Renaissance revived the idea of man's independence. In Donatello's marvellous statue of the young David the figure stands proudly on its own. It was the first free-standing nude statue to be successfully cast since the days of ancient Greece.

Donatello also revived the Roman love of figures mounted on horseback —equestrian statues, which made the figure look even more important and proud. A fine example is his statue of the condottiere Gattamelata. Verrocchio made an even more dramatic statue of the condottiere Bartolommeo Colleoni which still stands in Venice. It is said that when Verrocchio had completed the model he was told that someone else was going to do the figure. He was so angry that he broke the horse's head and legs and only repaired the model and finished the statue when the Venetians apologized.

In their garden in Florence, the Medici encouraged sculpture by starting a school for training young sculptors. It was there that Michelangelo learnt some of his

Left: Ghiberti's *Gates of Paradise* for the Florence Baptistry, with lifelike reliefs.

Three very different styles of Renaissance sculpture.
Left: Donatello's *David* is a delicately beautiful figure.

Below: Michelangelo's *David* is very powerful. The sculptor has emphasized the muscular strength of the body. The figure is nearly five metres high.

Right: Michelangelo never finished this almost melting figure of the dying Christ in the Rondanini *Pietà*.

skill. He showed his enthusiasm when he was quite young. There is a story that he carved the head of an old faun. Lorenzo de Medici passed by and pointed out that an old man would probably not have a full set of teeth. Immediately Michelangelo knocked out one or two of the teeth with his chisel and Lorenzo was delighted.

Michelangelo soon proved that he understood the strength and flow of the human form. You can see his skill in the confidence and youth of his statue of *David* at Florence, in the flowing drapery and detail of his *Pietà* at St Peter's and in the brooding anger on the face of his *Moses*. Later his style changed to the soft, almost melting shape of the *Dying Slave* and the oddly stretched

shape of his Rondanini *Pietà*. This style is known as Mannerism. It is characterized by very distorted, rather than realistic, figures.

In the north of Europe sculpture never became so free and confident during the Renaissance. On the whole it continued to be used as decoration and most of it was still done in relief for churches and cathedrals. But, as in northern painting, some of the figures became quite realistic. Claus Sluter produced some wonderfully lifelike characters for a group of prophets that he carved around the base of a large crucifix at Dijon. The figures are part of the Moses Fountain. But in the north there was never the feeling of pride in the human body that the Italian sculptures revived from the past.

Perfect Proportions

Most of the important and interesting buildings during the Middle Ages were castles and churches. The castles were built solidly for defence against knights and barbarians but the great cathedrals that were built toward the end of the Middle Ages were beautifully decorated with stone carvings. Their spires seem to reach toward heaven.

Renaissance churches were very different. They were much more simple. Instead of ornate carvings and pointed arches and spires, they had rounded domes and straight, upright columns. Instead of giving a very busy appearance, with lots of detail and angles, they appeared pleasantly balanced, with rectangles, squares and curves, just like the buildings of

ancient Rome. As in everything else, the Renaissance was copying the past.

There were many Roman ruins in Italy from which the Italians could learn. Brunelleschi went to Rome with his friend Donatello after he lost the competition with Ghiberti for designing the bronze doors in Florence. He carefully drew every piece of old Roman column and building he could find.

From his drawings and measurements, Brunelleschi formed a good idea of how the Romans constructed their arches and domes. He put his ideas into practice when he built the *cupola*, or dome, of the cathedral of Sta. Maria del Fiore in Florence. The church was so large that no other architect had been able to design a

dome to cover it. Brunelleschi nearly did not get the job because he refused to show anyone his plans before he started. He said that if they saw his model, the other architects would be able to build the dome, too. They allowed him to go ahead and he finished the commission.

Some of the Renaissance churches were quite small and look light and delicate. Brunelleschi built one such little church for the Pazzi family in Florence and Bramante built another little temple, or Tempietto, in Rome. But the Renaissance architects did not only build churches. They also built palaces and private houses in the style of ancient Rome. Some of the palaces were quite plain, like the one that was commissioned for the Pitti family. Others had columns in relief to decorate the facade, like the one that Alberti built for the Rucellai. In Venice, the library of San Marco had a very ornate facade with different kinds of columns, balustrades, garlands and sculptures.

There were plenty of opportunities for architects to try out their grand ideas. Pope Julius II decided to rebuild Rome to restore it to its old glory. He commissioned Bramante to rebuild the old church of St Peter's in 1506. Bramante's designs were too ambitious and expensive and the first dome that he planned for the church would certainly have collapsed. When Bramante died, Michelangelo took over the design and solved the problem of supporting the weight of the dome by making a double shell so that it would be lighter. The inner shell was made of wood and the outer shell of wood and lead. Michelangelo's dome still stands.

Many of the villas and palaces of the Renaissance do not look very comfortable in which to live. The architects seemed more concerned that they should look impressive.

Certainly that style of architecture, with its open columns and courtyards,

Left: The interior of the little church that Brunelleschi built for the Pazzi family in Florence.

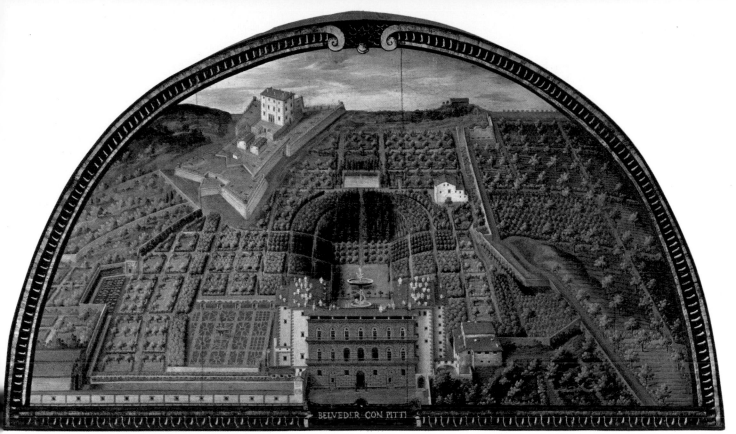

Above: This view of the original
Pitti Palace shows the fine
proportions of the building in its
magnificent grounds.

Right: Bramante's design for the
dome of St Peter's and, beyond,
the design by Michelangelo that
was used.

Below right: The light arches and
columns of the Foundling
Hospital in Florence show good
Renaissance design.

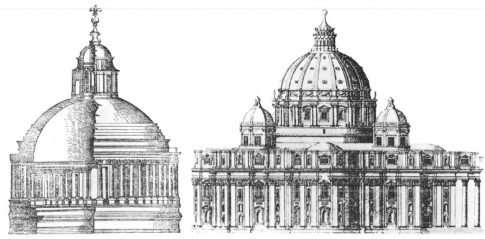

did not suit the cold, wet climate of
northern Europe. At first, the only
effect the Renaissance had in the
north was to add a certain amount of
decoration to local styles. In France,
Italian architects were employed by
Francis I to decorate Fontainebleau
and some *châteaux*, or castles, in the
Loire. In England, Henry VIII
employed sculptors from Florence to
decorate the Nonsuch Palace, which
was later destroyed. Hampton Court,
near London, also shows signs of
Renaissance style. And in Russia, an
architect from Milan built one of the
gates of the Kremlin. But it was long
after the Italian Renaissance that their
style in architecture really began to
influence architects in England and
other countries.

The End of the Age

The Renaissance spanned several centuries and it reached its peak in Italy in the 15th and early 16th centuries. But after that, ideas began to change quite rapidly. Art became more experimental and exaggerated the emotions of the subject as well as the physical characteristics. Scientists rebelled against the teachings of the classical writers and produced theories based on their own observations.

The Italian states and their rich rulers became politically weaker. At the end of the 15th century the French invaded Italy. The control of the smaller city states passed to larger powers such as France and the Papal States. They lost much of their individual character and influence. The Italian princes could no longer afford to maintain their lavish courts and patronages.

There was a greater interest in the fate of the common people, instead of just the wealthy and noble. The growing antagonism towards the riches and power of the popes came to a head with Luther's movement to reform the Church. His cause was taken up by the people in northern Europe who were tired of interference from a foreign pope in another country. Their beliefs became known as *Protestantism*—because they protested against the attitudes of the Church. Within a few years the religious unity of Europe was split between the Protestants of the North and the Catholics under the leadership of the Pope in Rome. Soon after, the Catholics fought back with their own counter-reformation, spearheaded by a special order—the Jesuits. They were formed to spread Catholic teaching and to restore faith in the Pope. Pope Paul IV ordered the nudes in Michelangelo's *Last Judgement* to be covered with drapes to prove that the Church had cleaned itself of all past scandal and corruption. It was a strange end to the Italian Renaissance.

Yet the Renaissance can truly be called a golden age. It saw a great flourish of activity in the arts and sciences. It produced buildings and works of art that are still regarded as marvellous. Millions of visitors every year still admire the splendour of cities such as Venice and Florence. At the same time it also provided a starting point for the exciting age of discovery in science and technology that followed.

The influence of the Italian Renaissance spread through Europe. The form which it took varied, but always it made people aware of the world around them and of their own important place in that world.

Right: Brunelleschi's dome still stands on the Cathedral in modern Florence, as a memorial to the spirit of the Renaissance.

Below: Not so enduring—*The Last Supper* deteriorated even in Leonardo's lifetime. Pollution now accelerates its decay.

Lifelines

Cesare Borgia
(1475-1507)

When Cesare's father became Pope Alexander VI, Cesare became a cardinal, but later gave up the church to take command of his father's armies. He quickly won a reputation as a successful military commander but he used treason, murder and intrigue to gain his victories rather than military skill. He also used the marriages of his sister, Lucrezia Borgia, as another means to increase the power of the Papal States. His ruthless tactics and cruelty in gaining his ends made him the model for Macchiavelli's book *The Prince*. However, when Alexander VI died, Cesare lost much of his power because the next pope, Julius II, was an enemy of the Borgias. Cesare was killed at a siege when he was only 32.

Peter Breughel
(about 1525-69)

Breughel was one of the most famous of the northern painters. He entered the Antwerp painter's guild in 1551. Twelve years later he moved to Brussels where he stayed until he died. Breughel loved painting large scenes of people in their environment. As he grew older he concentrated more and more on the people themselves. His paintings show how people survived the pettiness and harshness of everyday life. Although he himself was a cultivated townsman, the characters in his paintings are usually peasants, full of energy and humour, sometimes simple and sometimes cruel. His painting was influenced by another northern painter, Hieronymous Bosch.

Filippo Brunelleschi
(1377-1446)

He was born in Florence and trained as a sculptor. After he lost the competition with Ghiberti for the commission to design the doors for the Baptistry in Florence, Brunelleschi went with his friend Donatello to Rome. There they measured and drew all the ancient ruins they could. The two became laughingly known as 'the treasure seekers'. When he returned to Florence, Brunelleschi eventually won the commission to build the dome of the Cathedral. This was probably his greatest work. He supervised every detail of the construction and decoration himself. Brunelleschi's ideas on classical architecture greatly influenced artists as well as architects and he became a key Renaissance figure.

Nicolaus Copernicus
(1473-1543)

Copernicus was a Polish scholar who travelled to Rome, Padua and Bologna to acquire all the knowledge of the day on mathematics and astronomy. He returned to his home country where he studiously made his own observations of the stars over many years. He also carefully read ancient Greek and Arab books on astronomy. The popular notion of his time was that the sun went round the Earth. In his famous book, *On the Revolutions of Celestial Spheres*, Copernicus suggested that it was the other way round, that the sun, not the Earth, was the centre of the Universe. He discovered that Greek philosophers had suggested this as far back as the 3rd century BC. There was great opposition to his book.

Donatello
(1386-1466)

Donatello was the son of a member of the Florentine wool-carder's guild. Donatello probably learnt sculpture from the stonemasons working on Florence Cathedral. His earliest work was a marble statue of David, in 1408/9. His statues of St Mark and St George were the first two Renaissance statues to stand unsupported against a wall. Later he worked in bronze and his famous *David* was the first large-scale, free-standing nude of the Renaissance. In fact it was the first such bronze to be cast since classical times. Among his other works he also did a large equestrian statue which inspired all subsequent equestrian statues. Towards the end of his life, he began to carve in wood.

↑

Albrecht Dürer
(1471-1528)

→

Dürer was born in Nuremberg and trained in his father's goldsmith's workshop. He paid two long visits to Venice and later worked for seven years for the Emperor Maximilian I in Nuremberg, where for some of those years he received a fixed annual salary of 100 guilders. He exchanged works with the Italian painter Raphael and also travelled to Antwerp where he met the northern artist Grunewald. His earliest known work is a self-portrait which he completed when he was 13. He became the greatest German Renaissance painter, engraver and woodcut designer. He excelled in drawings which are starkly realistic, yet often symbolic, such as the portrait of his mother and *Knight, Death and the Devil*.

Desiderius Erasmus
(1466-1536)

↑

Erasmus was born in Rotterdam or Gouda and was the illegitimate son of a priest. He became a priest himself in 1492 but was primarily interested in scholarship and study. He became the most influential humanist thinker and writer of the northern Renaissance, and he wrote only in Latin and Greek. In 1516 he produced an edition of the New Testament with the original Greek text alongside his own Latin translation, which he dedicated to Pope Leo X. Among his best known works are *Adagia*, a collection of proverbs, and *Familiar Sayings*, a satire on contemporary manners. He travelled widely and talked to most of the important people in Europe. He grumbled a lot about the places he visited.

Isabella d'Este
(**1474-1539**)

Isabella d'Este came from a very wealthy and influential family. Her father was Ercole I, Duke of Ferrara, one of the most brilliant and prosperous courts of Europe. One of her brothers, Alfonso, was married to Lucrezia Borgia—a political marriage to save the lands of Ferrara from being seized by Cesare Borgia and Pope Alexander VI. Her sister, Beatrice, married Ludovico Sforza. Isabella herself married Francesco Gonzaga, marquis of Mantua. Both Isabella and Beatrice were rich and well-educated.

Their intelligence and artistic appreciation made them important patrons of the arts and they encouraged people such as Bramante, Leonardo da Vinci, Mantegna, Raphael and Titian. Isabella also helped her husband to guide the political fortunes of Mantua.

Marsilio Ficino
(**1433-99**)

Ficino was born near Florence and given early encouragement by Cosimo de Medici. Later he taught the young Lorenzo de Medici. He was ordained as a priest and became an official of

Florence Cathedral. Ficino was an admirer of the Greek philosopher Plato and he interpreted Plato's ideas to Renaissance scholars. He was a key figure of the Platonic Academy in Florence and he undertook the first complete translation of Plato into Latin; his translation was used for more than 200 years. He also interpreted the ideas of the Roman philosopher Plotinus. Ficino's methods of teaching were through informal discussions and courses. He believed that man would grow to love God more by understanding the potential of his own spirit.

Giotto
(**1266/7-1337**)

Giotto was born near Florence and regarded as the first of the great Italian painters of the Renaissance. He was taught by the artist Cimabue and he worked in Assisi, Rome, Padua, Florence and Naples, where he was appointed a *familiar*, or member of the royal household, in 1330. In 1334 he was appointed to be the supervisor of Florence Cathedral and architect to the city, not because he had any reputation as an architect but because of his fame as a painter. His paintings are important and interesting because the characters in them seem to be real people acting out the drama of religious stories. These contrasted with the religious paintings of the Middle Ages which had been flat and lifeless.

Johann Gutenberg
(**1396-1468**) →

Gutenberg was born in Mainz. He trained as a goldsmith, when he learnt his skill in metalwork. He was exiled from his home and went to Strasbourg but later returned to Mainz. Gutenberg can be said to have been the inventor of western printing. He introduced various elements that had not existed in the earlier eastern printing of China and Korea. He perfected the use of moveable type which made possible the use of the printing press on a mass scale. He and some colleagues started the printing of the famous 42-line Bible, which was finished in 1456. Gutenberg constantly ran into debt and had to be bought out by one of the partners. He died a poor man.

Julius II
(**1443-1513**) ↑

Giuliano della Rovere became a Franciscan monk and was made a Cardinal by his uncle, Pope Sixtus IV. In 1503 he became Pope Julius II. He restored the military strength of the Papacy and secured the Papal States against France and Venice. Julius was also one of the greatest of the Renaissance patrons. He commissioned the rebuilding of St Peter's in Rome in 1506 and he commissioned Michelangelo to paint the ceiling of

the Sistine Chapel. Michelangelo later sculpted several figures for Julius's tomb. But Julius was also interested in the Church. He created bishoprics in the West Indies and he sent missionaries to India and Africa.

Leo X
(**1475-1521**) ↓

Giovanni de Medici was the second son of Lorenzo de Medici. He succeeded Julius II as Pope Leo X in 1513 and faced the same political problems as his predecessor in maintaining the power of the Papal States against France and Venice. He

failed to plan a crusade against the Turks, who then captured Belgrade. Although he was a religious man, he failed to understand the need for reform in the Church. His quarrel with Luther grew into a bitter struggle and he excommunicated Luther in 1521. He gave King Henry VIII of England the title of *Defender of the Faith*. Leo spent lavishly on art and architecture. He continued with the rebuilding of St Peter's, under Raphael.

Martin Luther
(**1483-1546**) ↑

Luther went to school at Mansfeld, in Saxony. His father encouraged him to become a lawyer but he chose to become an Augustinian friar. He continued with advanced studies and lectured on religious subjects. In 1510 he went to Rome and was shocked by the wealth and hypocrisy of the Church there. He was particularly angered by the sale of indulgences to raise money for the Church, and nailed his 95 theses against such practices to the door of the All Saints' Church in Wittenberg. This provoked a quarrel with the Pope which brought about Luther's excommunication and started the move to reform the Church. Luther also translated the Bible into German for the first time and published many pamphlets. He was the best selling author of his time.

ceiling of the Sistine Chapel and the *Last Judgement* behind the altar, and his sculptures of *David*, the two *Dying Slaves*, the three *Pietà* and figures for the tombs of Julius II and the Medici.

Thomas More (1478-1535) →

More was born in London, the son of a judge, who forced him to study law. He also studied Greek and Latin. He became a humanist scholar, a pacifist,

Niccolò Macchiavelli (1469-1527) ↑

Born in Florence, Macchiavelli was given an important public office there when he was only 29. He went on several diplomatic missions to France and also negotiated with Cesare Borgia on behalf of Florence. Macchiavelli was an enthusiastic Florentine patriot, as well as a very able diplomat. He became the right-hand man to the Florentine head of state and led his own band of soldiers against Pisa. He was thrown out of Florence when the Medici returned in 1512. His famous book *The Prince*, partly based on the model of Cesare Borgia, was dedicated to the Medici in the hope of a reprieve. But he died a disappointed man.

Michelangelo Buonarroti (1475-1564) →

Michelangelo's mother died when he was six. He went to Florence when he was about 10 and at 13 he became an apprentice in the workshop of Domenique Ghirlandaio. He went on to the School of Sculpture in the Medici Gardens under the tutorship of Bertoldo di Giovanni, a pupil of Donatello. Here, he studied Greek and Roman marbles and listened to the teachings of Ficino in Lorenzo de Medici's palace. Most of his life was spent in Florence and Rome. He finally left Florence for Rome when he was 60. Michelangelo was the greatest sculptor of the Renaissance and his paintings rank with those of Leonardo and Raphael. His greatest works include the frescoes on the

and a reformer. Among his many achievements, Thomas More was a pioneer of women's education in England. In 1516 he wrote *Utopia*, the picture of an ideal state. He was a friend of Erasmus, Holbein and Henry VIII. More succeeded Wolsey as Lord Chancellor of England but later quarrelled with Henry over his marriage to Anne Boleyn. He refused to acknowledge Henry as Head of the Church. As a result, he was imprisoned in the Tower of London and executed.

Raphael ➡
(1483-1520)
He was born in Urbino, the son of a mediocre painter, and enjoyed the atmosphere of the court of the Montefeltros. He became a friend of Castiglione and later painted his portrait. In 1504, Raphael went to Florence and studied Leonardo and Michelangelo. Four years later he was encouraged to go to Rome by Bramante and he received commissions for paintings from Pope Julius II. Later, Leo X commissioned tapestries for the walls of the Sistine Chapel, for which Raphael did the cartoons. Although he died when he was only 37, Raphael is one of the greatest artists of the Renaissance.

Titian ➡
(1487/90-1576)
Titian is recognized as the greatest Venetian painter of the Renaissance. He trained in the shops of Gentile and Giovanni Bellini and was very influenced by Giorgione for a short time. One of his patrons was Alfonso d'Este, Duke of Ferrara, for whom he painted his famous *Bacchus and Ariadne*. Many of his paintings were of religious or mythological subjects and these are full of colour and vitality. In the 1530s he started to paint a great many portraits, including portraits of the Emperor Charles V and King Francis I of France. He became court painter to Charles V and was knighted by him. Later he painted for Charles's son, Philip, King of Spain. He also visited Rome and painted Pope Paul III.

Paolo Uccello
(1397-1475)
Uccello was born in Florence, the son of a barber-surgeon. He became a member of Ghiberti's studio and then moved to Venice where he worked on mosaics for about five years. He returned to Florence in 1431 and later painted the effigy of Sir John Hawkwood, the English condottiere, in Florence Cathedral. He also spent some years in Padua. Uccello's paintings were influenced by Donatello and by the theories on architecture and perspective of Alberti. His most famous paintings are the three large battle scenes of the *Rout of San Romano* (1456), which were commissioned by Cosimo de Medici. Decorative detail, landscape and perspective are all important in these paintings.

Datelines

EUROPE

Gunpowder invented
1313

HUNDRED YEARS' WAR 1337-1453

**WAR OF
THE ROSES
1445-1485**

Small cannon perfected
1320

Black Death
reaches Europe
1347

Ascent of Medici in Florence

Black Death kills a third
of England's population
1349

First spectacles
1285

Black death re-appears
in England
1361

Movable printing type
invented about 1450

First printed music 1465

Giotto 1266-1337

Ghiberti 1378-1455

First book in English
printed 147.

Production of
stained glass windows
1300

Fra Angelico 1387-1455

Uccello 1397-1475

Oil paints invented
1350-1400

Leonardo da Vinci 1452-1519

Weaving in England
1331

ASIA/AFRICA

**CHINA UNDER
THE MONGOLS 1297-1368**

THE OTTOMAN TURKS
Constantinople captured by Turks 1453

Portuguese begin exploring
African coast 1415

AMERICA

INCA EMPIRE 1200-1532

Aztecs establish Mexico City 1327

Defeat of Spanish Armada
1588   **ENGLISH CIVIL WAR**
1642-1646

Battle of Ravenna:
French driven from Italy
1512   Earthquake in London 1580

THIRTY YEARS' WAR
1618-1648

HENRY VII
RULES ENGLAND
1485-1509

Telescope invented
1608

Elizabeth I comes to throne
1558

HENRY VIII
RULES ENGLAND
1509-1547

First fire engines in England
1625

First postal service between
London and Edinburgh
1635

Beginning of Reformation 1517

Luther excommunicated 1521

Reformation in Switzerland 1525

Tea first drunk in England
1650

ürer 1471-1528

Reformation in France 1532

Michelangelo 1475-1564

Jesuit Society founded 1534

Great Plague of London 1665

Raphael 1483-1520

Reformation in Scotland 1541

Fire of London 1666

Coffee first brought
to England 1517

Protestantism allowed in Germany
1555

Suleiman the Great
becomes Sultan of Turkey
1520

WAR BETWEEN PERSIA AND TURKEY
1602-1627

MING DYNASTY 1368-1644

Europeans expelled from
China 1523

Jesuit missionaries
in China 1582

Cortés captures Mexico City from Aztecs 1521
Columbus crosses Atlantic 1492
Cabot discovers North America 1497

First printing press
in North America 1639

Glossary

Abacus: Calculating frame for simple mathematics; also a course in mathematics.

Alchemist: Person who uses supposedly magical chemistry to turn ordinary metals into gold.

Apothecary: Pharmacist who prepares medicinal drugs.

Apprentice: Learner of a craft, who works for a master in exchange for instruction.

Astrolabe: Instrument for measuring the altitude of the sun and stars, used in navigation.

Astrologer: Person who studies the stars to predict the future.

Cassone: Marriage chest, often richly decorated.

City State: An area containing several towns and cities controlled by one powerful independent city.

Condottiere: Military captain heading mercenary army, with contract, or *condotta*, to fight for certain cities or princes.

Cours d'amour: French courts of love, groups who discussed poetry and chivalry.

Crusade: Christian military expedition against Turks and Moors in Holy Land.

Cupola: A small dome forming a roof.

Dance of Death: Also *Danse Macabre*; illustrations, usually in woodcut, showing skeletons leading rich and poor to their death.

Dowry: Money paid by the family of the girl to the man she is marrying or to his family.

Excommunication: To cut someone off from membership of the Church.

Guild: An association of craftsmen formed for mutual benefit and protection.

Heretic: Person who holds a religious belief that goes against the teaching of the Catholic Church.

Herbal: Books on herbs and their uses as medicine.

Humanism: Study of Greek and Roman art and thought with emphasis on the qualities of man.

Indulgence: Pardon for sins; indulgences were usually sold to raise money for the Church.

Inquisition: Court for trying heretics, which used torture to obtain confession and then dealt cruel punishments.

Journeyman: Worker who has finished his apprenticeship and works on a daily or contract basis.

L'uomo universale: The universal man; the Renaissance ideal, outlined by Castiglione in *The Courtier*, of the man who was good at everything.

Mercenary: Professional soldier, usually foreign, who fights for profit not for loyalty to country.

Monopoly: Exclusive right to a particular trade, to protect that trade from competition.

Mystery play: Dramatic retelling of religious story, popular in Middle Ages and Renaissance.

Pageant: Series of scenes showing episodes in a religious or historical story.

Patron: Wealthy person who commissions work from artists of many kinds and often houses them.

Perspective: The apparent relative size of objects as they grow smaller in the distance; method of showing this in flat paintings.

Philosopher's stone: The secret substance that alchemists believed would turn everything into gold.

Pieta: Figure of the Virgin Mary mourning over Christ's dead body.

Pilgrimage: Journey to a holy place or shrine.

Propaganda: Information intended to persuade people to a particular point of view.

Quadrant: Instrument shaped like a quarter circle for measuring angles of stars for navigation.

Reformation: Movement to reform the Church, which resulted in the rise of Protestantism, and was followed by the Catholic *Counter Reformation*.

Relics: Part of the body or possessions of a holy person, kept as an object to worship.

Relief: Figures and scenes carved so that they stand out from a flat surface.

Sfumato: Technique of blurred shading in painting used by Leonardo da Vinci.

Stucco: Plaster on wall decorated in relief.

Tempera: Powdered colours bound with egg-yolk, a common form of paint before oil-paint.

Vagabond: Wanderer with no home or job.

Vernacular: The native language of a particular people.

Woodcut: Wooden block on which a picture or letter design has been cut, used for printing.

Index